TILL WE *Meet*
AGAIN

TILL WE *Meet*

AGAIN

SELECTED BY

SHERSTA CHABOT

WORDS *of*

COMFORT AND HOPE

for the

GRIEVING

PLAIN SIGHT PUBLISHING

AN IMPRINT OF CEDAR FORT, INC.

SPRINGVILLE, UTAH

ISBN 13: 978-1-4621-1205-0

Published by Plain Sight Publishing, an imprint of Cedar Fort, Inc.
2373 W. 700 S., Springville, UT 84663
Distributed by Cedar Fort, Inc., www.cedarfort.com

   Library of Congress Cataloging-in-Publication Data on File

Cover design by Angela D. Olsen
Cover design © 2013 by Lyle Mortimer
Edited and typeset by Whitney Lindsley

Printed in the United States of America

10 9 8 7 6 5 4 3 2 1

For all those left behind

OTHER BOOKS BY

Shersta Chabot

The Symbols of Christmas

Contents

Foreword

American poet Alice Cary (1820–1871) writes:

> *My soul is full of whispered song,—*
> *My blindness is my sight;*
> *The shadows that I feared so long*
> *Are full of life and light.*

When death casts its shadow over our lives, it often brings us a profound sense of loss and grief. We naturally fear the mysterious force that causes such a finite end. But as Alice Cary illustrates, those fearful shadows may simply be the prelude to a place of light, a place that is filled with a new kind of life.

Titled "Dying Hymn," Cary's beautiful verse describes a passing from mortality that sets the tone for this collection of best-loved poems, quotations, and prayers of comfort and hope. Selected for the variety and the beauty of the messages conveyed, each work speaks to the grief that forms a common tie between those of us who have lost a loved one, and at the same time celebrates the life that was, and is, the life that holds us close and stays in our hearts no matter the time or space that divides us.

Preface

WORDS *of* COMFORT

In times of grief, it can be difficult to know what to say or do. Those experiencing the painful loss of a loved one may be as uncertain as those trying to extend their sympathies or support. Because we each experience and react to events in our lives in uniquely personal ways, there are no perfectly right or wrong words for every circumstance. However, do not let uncertainty intimidate you into silence or avoidance. Any expression of genuine concern, including simply offering a listening ear, will be helpful.

Other ways to express your love and support include:

- Allow grieving individuals to express their feelings without pushing or trying to argue with them. This is not the time to attempt to control the expression of their grief. They may also want to "tell the story," even multiple times, about how their loved one died. This retelling is an important part of acknowledgement and acceptance, and can be gently encouraged.

- Acknowledge the grieving person's pain.

- ❧ Really listen, and make yourself available to listen, as needed.

- ❧ Talk about the person that has passed on, if the grieving person desires.

- ❧ If appropriate, communicate your love with a gentle hug.

- ❧ Make specific offers of help and, on acceptance, follow up with action

- ❧ When speaking, keep it simple. Do not try to be conversational. Statements like: "I am so sorry," "My thoughts and prayers are with you," "I admired him or her because . . . ," and even "I don't know what to say, but just know that I love you" will communicate your love and support without overwhelming or offending.

On the other hand, unhelpful or unwelcome comments can and will make a difficult situation worse. For example, statements like "It was God's will," "You're strong enough to handle this," or "I know how you feel" may cause more resentment and anxiety than comfort. Additionally, statements such as "Be grateful for the time you had with him or her," "Be grateful for the children/loved ones you still have," or even "You should be over this/shouldn't be feeling this way" will invalidate and minimize the other person's pain and suffering, and may add to his or her burden by prompting guilt or frustration over their inability to meet your expectations.

Perhaps this is why we so often turn to the beautiful language of poetry and other eloquent writing—to help us express what are, by definition, the inexpressible feelings that accompany a great loss. When the words escape us, we can turn to those of others who have gone before, writers and speakers and poets who have attempted to capture the often indescribable and elusive emotions of grief and sorrow—and love. For just a little while, perhaps we may find a kind of solace between the lines of the verses, quotations, and eulogies collected here in this book.

Whether we seek to comfort others or seek some comfort of our own, let the soothing rhythms and rhymes of beautiful language speak to us, around us, and through us.

Part 1

IN MEMORIAM: HONORING
and REMEMBERING
LIVES *and* LOVES

The heart hath its own memory, like the mind. And in it are enshrined the precious keepsakes, into which is wrought the giver's loving thought.

Henry Wadsworth Longfellow (1807–1882)
FROM HIS POEM "FROM MY ARM-CHAIR"

To live in hearts we leave behind is not to die.

Thomas Campbell (1777–1844)

To die completely, a person must not only forget but be forgotten, and he who is not forgotten is not dead.

Samuel Butler (1835–1902)

REMEMBER
Christina Georgina Rossetti (1830–1894)

Remember me when I am gone away,
Gone far away into the silent land;
When you can no more hold me by the hand,
Nor I half turn to go yet turning stay.
Remember me when no more day by day
You tell me of our future that you planned:
Only remember me; you understand
It will be late to counsel then or pray.
Yet if you should forget me for a while
And afterwards remember, do not grieve:
For if the darkness and corruption leave
A vestige of the thoughts that once I had,
Better by far you should forget and smile
Than that you should remember and be sad.

Sweet is the memory of departed friends. Like the mellow rays of the declining sun, it falls tenderly, yet sadly, on the heart.

Washington Irving (1783–1859)

It is not length of life, but depth of life.

Ralph Waldo Emerson (1803–1882)

When you were born, you cried and the world rejoiced. Live your life in a manner so that when you die the world cries and you rejoice.

Native American proverb

from FAREWELL
Anne Brontë (1820–1849)

Farewell to thee! but not farewell
To all my fondest thoughts of thee:
Within my heart they still shall dwell;
And they shall cheer and comfort me.

O, beautiful, and full of grace!
If thou hadst never met mine eye,
I had not dreamed a living face
Could fancied charms so far outvie. . . .

Adieu, but let me cherish still
The hope with which I cannot part.
Contempt may wound, and coldness chill,
But still it lingers in my heart.

And who can tell but Heaven, at last,
May answer all my thousand prayers,
And bid the future pay the past
With joy for anguish, smiles for tears?

Earth has one angel less, and heaven one more since yesterday. Already, kneeling at the throne, she has received her welcome, and is resting on the bosom of her Saviour.

Nathaniel Hawthorne (1804–1864)

You will not see me, so you must have faith. I wait for the time when we can soar together again, both aware of each other. Until then, live your life to its fullest and when you need me, just whisper my name in your heart, . . . I will be there.

Emily Dickinson (1830–1886)

from ON THE DEATH OF
MY SON CHARLES
Daniel Webster (1792–1852)

My son, thou wast my heart's delight,
Thy morn of life was gay and cheery;
That morn has rushed to sudden night,
Thy father's house is sad and dreary.

I held thee on my knee, my son!
And kissed thee laughing, kissed thee weeping;
But ah! thy little day is done,
Thou 'rt with thy angel sister sleeping.
Dear Angel, thou art safe in heaven;

No prayers for thee need more be made;
Oh! let thy prayers for those be given
Who oft have blessed thy infant head.

from THE GIAOUR

Lord George Gordon Noel Byron (1788–1824)

She was a form of life and light—
That seen—became a part of sight,
And rose—where'er I turn'd mine eye—
The Morning-star of Memory!
Yes, Love indeed is light from heaven—
A spark of that immortal fire
With angels shar'd—by Alla given,
To lift from earth our low desire.

ON THE RELIGIOUS MEMORY OF MRS. CATHERINE THOMSON

John Milton (1608–1674)

When Faith and Love, which parted from thee never,
Had ripen'd thy just soul to dwell with God,
Meekly thou didst resign this earthly load
Of death, called life, which us from life doth sever.
Thy works, and alms, and all thy good endeavour,
Stay'd not behind, nor in the grave were trod;
But, as Faith pointed with her golden rod,
Follow'd thee up to joy and bliss for ever.
Love led them on; and Faith, who knew them best
Thy handmaids, clad them o'er with purple beams
And azure wings, that up they flew so drest,
And spake the truth of thee in glorious themes
Before the Judge; who thenceforth bid thee rest,
And drink thy fill of pure immortal streams.

from TO SIR G. H. B. UPON THE DEATH OF HIS SISTER-IN-LAW

William Wordsworth (1770–1850)

O for a dirge! But why complain?
Ask rather a triumphal strain
When Fermor's race is run;
A garland of immortal boughs
To twine around the Christian's brows,
Whose glorious work is done.

We pay a high and holy debt;
No tears of passionate regret
Shall stain this votive lay;
Ill-worthy, Beaumont! were the grief
That flings itself on wild relief
When Saints have passed away.

Sad doom, at Sorrow's shrine to kneel,
For ever covetous to feel,
And impotent to bear!
Such once was hers—to think and think
On severed love, and only sink
From anguish to despair!

But nature to its inmost part
Faith had refined; and to her heart
A peaceful cradle given:
Calm as the dew-drop's, free to rest
Within a breeze-fanned rose's breast
Till it exhales to Heaven. . . .

Thou takest not away, O Death!
Thou strikest—absence perisheth,
Indifference is no more;
The future brightens on our sight;
For on the past hath fallen a light
That tempts us to adore.

It is an exquisite and beautiful thing in our nature that when the heart is touched and softened by some tranquil happiness or affectionate feeling, the memory of the "dead" comes over it most powerfully and irresistibly. It would seem almost as though our better thoughts and sympathies were charms, in virtue of which the soul is enabled to hold some vague and mysterious intercourse with the spirits of those whom we dearly loved in life. Alas! how often and how long may those patient angels hover around us, watching for the spell which is so seldom uttered, and so soon forgotten!

Charles Dickens (1812–1870)

A SONG BEFORE GRIEF

Rose Hawthorne Lathrop (1851–1926)

Sorrow, my friend,
When shall you come again?
The wind is slow, and the bent willows send
Their silvery motions wearily down the plain.
The bird is dead
That sang this morning through the summer rain!

Sorrow, my friend,
I owe my soul to you.
And if my life with any glory end
Of tenderness for others, and the words are true,
Said, honoring, when I 'm dead,—
Sorrow, to you, the mellow praise, the funeral wreath,
    are due.

And yet, my friend,
When love and joy are strong,
Your terrible visage from my sight I rend
With glances to blue heaven. Hovering along,
By mine your shadow led,
"Away!" I shriek, "nor dare to work my newsprung
    mercies wrong!"

Still, you are near:
Who can your care withstand?
When deep eternity shall look most clear,
Sending bright waves to kiss the trembling land,
My joy shall disappear,—
A flaming torch thrown to the golden sea
    by your pale hand.

SUCCESS

Bessie Stanley (1879–1952)

He has achieved success, who has lived well, laughed often,
    and loved much;
who has gained the respect of intelligent men and the love
    of little children;
who has filled his niche and accomplished his task;
who has left the world better than he found it,
whether by an improved poppy, a perfect poem, or a
    rescued soul;
who has never lacked appreciation of earth's beauty, or
    failed to express it;
who has always looked for the best in others and given the
    best he had;
whose life was an inspiration and
whose memory a benediction.

from ON THE DEATH OF QUEEN VICTORIA, 1901
Sir Wilfrid Laurier (1841–1919)

Undoubtedly we may find in history instances where death has caused perhaps more passionate outbursts of grief, but it is impossible to find instances where death has caused so universal, so sincere, so heartfelt an expression of sorrow. In the presence of these many evidences of grief . . . in the presence of so many tokens of admiration, where it is not possible to find a single discordant note . . . it is not too much to say that the grave has just closed upon one of the great characters of history.

What is greatness? We are accustomed to call great those exceptional beings upon whom heaven has bestowed some of its choicest gifts, which astonish and dazzle the world by the splendor of faculties, phenomenally developed, even when these faculties are much marred by defects and weaknesses which make them nugatory of the good.

But this is not, in my estimation at least, the highest conception of greatness. The equipoise of a well-balanced mind, the equilibrium of faculties well and evenly ordered, the luminous insight of a calm judgment, are gifts which are as rarely found in one human being as the possession of the more dazzling though less solid qualities. And when these high qualities are . . . combined with purity of soul, kindness of heart, generosity of disposition, elevation of purpose, and devotion to duty, this is what seems to me to be the highest conception of greatness. . . .

She is now no more—no more? Nay, I boldly say she lives—lives in the hearts of her subjects; lives in the pages of history. And as the ages revolve, as her pure profile stands more marked against the horizon of time, the verdict of posterity will ratify the judgment of those who were her subjects. She ennobled mankind; she exalted royalty; the world is better for her life.

I MEASURE EVERY GRIEF

Emily Dickinson (1830–1886)

I measure every grief I meet
With analytic eyes;
I wonder if it weighs like mine,
Or has an easier size.

I wonder if they bore it long,
Or did it just begin?
I could not tell the date of mine,
It feels so old a pain.

I wonder if it hurts to live,
And if they have to try,
And whether, could they choose between,
They would not rather die.

I wonder if when years have piled—
Some thousands — on the cause
Of early hurt, if such a lapse
Could give them any pause;

Or would they go on aching still
Through centuries above,
Enlightened to a larger pain
By contrast with the love.

The grieved are many, I am told;
The reason deeper lies,—
Death is but one and comes but once,
And only nails the eyes.

There's grief of want, and grief of cold, —
A sort they call 'despair;'
There's banishment from native eyes,
In sight of native air.

And though I may not guess the kind
Correctly, yet to me
A piercing comfort it affords
In passing Calvary,

To note the fashions of the cross,
Of those that stand alone,
Still fascinated to presume
That some are like my own.

If we have been pleased with life, we should not be displeased
with death, since it comes from the hand of the same master.

Michelangelo (1475–1564)

Yesterday is a memory,
tomorrow is a mystery,
and today is a gift—
which is why it is called the present.
What the caterpillar perceives is the end,
to the butterfly is just the beginning.
Everything that has a beginning
has an ending.

Buddhist saying

EPITAPH TO A FRIEND
Robert Burns (1759–1796)

An honest man here lies at rest
As e'er God with his image blest!
The friend of man, the friend of truth;
The friend of age, and guide of youth:
Few hearts like his, with virtue warm'd,
Few heads with knowledge so informed;
If there's another world, he lives in bliss;
If there is none, he made the best of this.

from DEATHS OF LITTLE CHILDREN
(James Henry) Leigh Hunt (1784–1859)

A Grecian philosopher being asked why he wept for the death of his son, since the sorrow was in vain, replied, "I weep on that account." And his answer became his wisdom.

There are griefs so gentle in their very nature that it would be worse than false heroism to refuse them a tear. Of this kind are the deaths of infants. . . . It is the nature of tears of this kind, however strongly they may gush forth, to run into quiet waters at last. We cannot easily, for the whole course of our lives, think with pain of any good and kind person whom we have lost. It is the divine nature of their qualities to conquer pain and death itself: to turn the memory of them into pleasure; to survive with a placid aspect in our imaginations. We are writing at this moment just opposite a spot which contains the grave of one inexpressibly dear to us. . . . And yet the sight of this spot does not give us pain. . . . Happiness was what its tenant, through all her troubles, would have diffused. To diffuse happiness and to enjoy it, is not only carrying on her wishes, but realizing her hopes.

Those who have lost an infant, are never, as it were, without an infant child. They are the only persons who, in one sense, retain it always, and they furnish their neighbours with the same idea. The other children grow up to manhood and womanhood, and suffer all the changes of mortality. This one alone is rendered an immortal child. Death has arrested it with his kindly harshness, and blessed it into an eternal image of youth and innocence.

Of such as these are the pleasantest shapes that visit our fancy and hopes. They are the ever-smiling emblems of joy; the prettiest pages that wait upon imagination. Lastly, "Of these are the kingdom of heaven." Wherever there is a province of that benevolent and all-accessible empire, whether on earth or elsewhere, such are the gentle spirits that must inhabit it.

We understand death for the first time when he puts his hand upon one whom we love.

Madame de Stael (1766–1817)

The burden becomes light that is shared by love.

Ovid (43 BC–AD 17)

WHILE WAITING FOR THEE

Helen Steiner Rice (1900–1981)

Don't weep at my grave,
For I am not there,
I've a date with a butterfly
To dance in the air.
I'll be singing in the sunshine,
Wild and free,
Playing tag with the wind,
While I'm waiting for thee.

THE COMFORT AND SWEETNESS
OF PEACE

Helen Steiner Rice (1900–1981)

After the clouds, the sunshine,
after the winter, the spring,
after the shower, the rainbow,
for life is a changeable thing.
After the night, the morning,
bidding all darkness cease,
after life's cares and sorrows,
the comfort and sweetness of peace.

from AT HIS BROTHER'S GRAVE, 1879

Robert Green Ingersoll (1833–1899)

The loved and loving brother, husband, father, friend, died where manhood's morning almost touches noon, and while the shadows still were falling toward the west.

He had not passed on life's highway the stone that marks the highest point, but being weary for a moment he lay down by the wayside, and, using his burden for a pillow, fell into that dreamless sleep that kisses down his eyelids still. While yet in love with life and raptured with the world, he passed to silence and pathetic dust.

Yet, after all, it may be best, just in the happiest, sunniest hour of all the voyage, while eager winds are kissing every sail, to dash against the unseen rock, and in an instant hear the billows roar above a sunken ship. For, whether in mid-sea or among the breakers of the farther shore, a wreck must mark at last the end of each and all. And every life, no matter if its every hour is rich with love, and every moment jeweled with a joy, will, at its close, become a tragedy, as sad, and deep, and dark as can be woven of the warp and woof of mystery and death. . . .

Life is a narrow vale between the cold and barren peaks of two eternities. We strive in vain to look beyond the heights. We cry aloud, and the only answer is the echo of our wailing cry. From the voiceless lips of the unreplying dead there comes no word; but in the night of death hope sees a star and listening love can hear the rustle of a wing.

O MY LOVE'S LIKE A RED, RED ROSE

Robert Burns (1759–1796)

O my Love's like a red, red rose,
That's newly sprung in June.
O, my Love's like the melody
That's sweetly played in tune.

As fair art thou, my bonnie lass,
So deep in love am I,
And I will love thee still, my dear,
Till all the seas go dry:

Till all the seas go dry, my dear,
And the rocks melt with the sun!
I will love thee still, my dear,
While the sands of life shall run.

And fare thee well, my only Love!
And fare thee well, a while!
And I will come again, my Love
Though it were ten thousand mile.*

*Note: Spelling standardized throughout

from BY EMERSON'S GRAVE, 1882
Walt Whitman (1819–1892)

So used are we to suppose a heroic death can only come from out of battle or storm, or mighty personal contest, or amid dramatic incidents or danger, (have we not been taught so for ages by all the plays and poems?) that few even of those who most sympathizingly mourn Emerson's late departure will fully appreciate the ripened grandeur of that event, with its play of calm and fitness, like evening light on the sea. . . .

We can say, as Abraham Lincoln at Gettysburg, It is not we who come to consecrate the dead—we reverently come to receive, if so it may be, some consecration to ourselves and daily work from him.

There are moments of life that we never forget, which brighten and brighten as time steals away.

J. G. Percival (1795–1858)

If human love hath power to penetrate the veil—and hath it not?—then there are yet living here a few who have the blessedness of knowing that an angel loves them.

Nathaniel Hawthorne (1804–1864)

MY DEAREST

Christina Georgina Rossetti (1830–1894)

When I am dead, my dearest,
Sing no sad songs for me;
Plant thou no roses at my head,
Nor shady cypress tree:
Be the green grass above me
With showers and dewdrops wet;
And if thou wilt, remember,
And if thou wilt, forget.

I shall not see the shadows,
I shall not feel the rain;
I shall not hear the nightingale
Sing on, as if in pain:
And dreaming through the twilight
That doth not rise nor set,
Haply I may remember,
And haply may forget.

I am waiting for you,
for an interval, somewhere very near,
just round the corner.

All is well.

from IN MEMORIAM
Alfred, Lord Tennyson (1809–1892)

Calm is the morn without a sound,
Calm as to suit a calmer grief,
And only thro' the faded leaf
The chestnut pattering to the ground:

Calm and deep peace in this wide air,
These leaves that redden to the fall;
And in my heart, if calm at all,
If any calm, a calm despair . . .

Thou comest, much wept for: such a breeze
Compell'd thy canvas, and my prayer
Was as the whisper of an air
To breathe thee over lonely seas.

For I in spirit saw thee move
Thro' circles of the bounding sky,
Week after week: the days go by:
Come quick, thou bringest all I love.

Henceforth, wherever thou mayst roam,
My blessing, like a line of light,
Is on the waters day and night,
And like a beacon guards thee home. . . .

Love is and was my Lord and King,
And in his presence I attend
To hear the tidings of my friend,
Which every hour his couriers bring.

Love is and was my King and Lord,
And will be, tho' as yet I keep
Within his court on earth, and sleep
Encompass'd by his faithful guard,

And hear at times a sentinel
Who moves about from place to place,
And whispers to the worlds of space,
In the deep night, that all is well.

Part 2

IN LUMINE: THE JOURNEY
from LIFE *to* LIGHT

The grave is but a covered bridge, leading from light to light, through a brief darkness.

Henry Wadsworth Longfellow (1807–1882)

Death and love are the two wings which bear man from earth to heaven.

Michelangelo (1475–1564)

IMMORTAL LOVE

George Edward Woodberry (1855–1930)

Immortal love, too high for my possessing,—
Yet, lower than thee, where shall I find repose?
Long in my youth I sang the morning rose,
By earthly things the heavenly pattern guessing!
Long fared I on, beauty and love caressing,
And finding in my heart a place for those
Eternal fugitives; the golden close
Of evening folds me, still their sweetness blessing.

Oh happy we, the first-born heirs of nature,
For whom the Heavenly Sun delays his light!
He by the sweets of every mortal creature
Tempers eternal beauty to our sight;
And by the glow upon love's earthly feature
Maketh the path of our departure bright.

from A LITTLE WHILE
Emily Brontë (1818–1848)

A little while, a little while,
The weary task is put away,
And I can sing and I can smile,
Alike, while I have holiday.

Where wilt thou go, my harassed heart—
What thought, what scene invites thee now
What spot, or near or far apart,
Has rest for thee, my weary brow? . . .

A heaven so clear, an earth so calm,
So sweet, so soft, so hushed an air;
And, deepening still the dreamlike charm,
Wild moor-sheep feeding everywhere.

O MAY I JOIN THE CHOIR INVISIBLE

George Eliot (1819–1880)

O may I join the choir invisible
Of those immortal dead who live again
In minds made better by their presence; live
In pulses stirr'd to generosity,
In deeds of daring rectitude, in scorn
Of miserable aims that end with self,
In thoughts sublime that pierce the night like stars,
And with their mild persistence urge men's minds
To vaster issues.

So to live is heaven:
To make undying music in the world,
Breathing a beauteous order that controls
With growing sway the growing life of man.
So we inherit that sweet purity
For which we struggled, fail'd and agoniz'd
With widening retrospect that bred despair.
Rebellious flesh that would not be subdued,
A vicious parent shaming still its child,
Poor anxious penitence is quick dissolv'd;
Its discords, quench'd by meeting harmonies,
Die in the large and charitable air;
And all our rarer, better, truer self,
That sobb'd religiously in yearning song,
That watch'd to ease the burthen of the world,
Laboriously tracing what must be,
And what may yet be better—saw rather
A worthier image for the sanctuary
And shap'd it forth before the multitude,
Divinely human, raising worship so

To higher reverence more mix'd with love—
That better self shall live till human Time
Shall fold its eyelids, and the human sky
Be gather'd like a scroll within the tomb
Unread forever.

This is life to come.
Which martyr'd men have made more glorious
For us who strive to follow.
May I reach
That purest heaven—be to other souls
The cup of strength in some great agony,
Enkindle generous ardor, feed pure love,
Beget the smiles that have no cruelty,
Be the sweet presence of a good diffus'd,
And in diffusion ever more intense!
So shall I join the choir invisible
Whose music is the gladness of the world.

from THE SLEEP

Elizabeth Barrett Browning (1806–1861)

Of all the thoughts of God that are
Borne inward into souls afar,
Along the Psalmist's music deep—
Now tell me if that any is,
For gift or grace, surpassing this—
"He giveth His beloved sleep?" . . .
His dews drop mutely on the hill;
His cloud above it saileth still,
Though on its slope men sow and reap.
More softly than the dew is shed,
Or cloud is floated overhead,
"He giveth His beloved, sleep." . . .

And, friends, dear friends—when it shall be
That this low breath is gone from me,
And round my bier ye come to weep—
Let one, most loving of you all,
Say, "Not a tear must o'er her fall—
'He giveth His beloved, sleep!'"

A LAMENT

Percy Bysshe Shelley (1792–1822)

O World! O Life! O Time!
On whose last steps I climb,
Trembling at that where I had stood before;
When will return the glory of your prime?
No more—Oh, never more!

Out of the day and night
A joy has taken flight:
Fresh spring, and summer, and winter hoar
Move my faint heart with grief, but with delight
No more—Oh, never more!

There is a sacredness in tears. They are not the mark of weakness, but of power. They speak more eloquently than ten thousand tongues.

Washington Irving (1783–1859)

Honest plain words best pierce the ear of grief.

William Shakespeare (1564–1616)

Great grief makes sacred those upon whom its hand is laid. Joy may elevate, ambition glorify, but sorrow alone can consecrate.

Horace Greeley (1811–1872)

BELIEVE AND TAKE HEART

John Lancaster Spalding (1840–1916)

What can console for a dead world?
We tread on dust which once was life;
To nothingness all things are hurled:
What meaning in a hopeless strife?
Time's awful storm
Breaks but the form.

Whatever comes, whatever goes,
Still throbs the heart whereby we live;
The primal joys still lighten woes,
And time which steals doth also give.
Fear not, be brave:
God can thee save.

The essential truth of life remains,
Its goodness and its beauty too,
Pure love's unutterable gains,
And hope which thrills us through and through:
God has not fled,
Souls are not dead.

Not in most ancient Palestine,
Nor in the lightsome air of Greece,
Were human struggles more divine,
More blessed with guerdon of increase:
Take thou thy stand
In the workers' band.

Hast then no faith? Thine is the fault:—
What prophets, heroes, sages, saints,
Have loved, on thee still makes assault,
Thee with immortal things acquaints.
On life then seize:
Doubt is disease.

from REST FOR THE SOUL

James Montgomery (1771–1854)

Return unto thy rest, my soul,
From all the wanderings of thy thought,
From sickness unto death made whole,
Safe through a thousand perils brought.

BE MINE

William Cox Bennett (1820–1895)

Be mine, and I will give thy name
To Memory's care,
So well, that it shall breathe, with fame,
Immortal air,
That time and change and death shall be
Scorn'd by the life I give to thee.

I will not, like the sculptor, trust
Thy shape to stone;
That, years shall crumble into dust,
Its form unknown;
No—the white statue's life shall be
Short, to the life I'll give to thee.

Not to the canvas worms may fret
Thy charms I'll give;
Soon shall the world those charms forget,
If there they live;
The life that colors lend shall be
Poor to the life I'll give to thee.

For thou shalt live, defying time
And mocking death,
In music on—O life sublime!—
A nation's breath;
Love, in a people's songs, shall be
The eternal life I'll give to thee.

He who has most of heart, knows most of sorrow.

Philip James Bailey (1816–1902)

It eases some, though none it ever cured, to think their sorrows others have endured.

William Shakespeare (1564–1616)

Here bring your wounded hearts, here tell your anguish: earth hath no sorrow that heaven cannot heal.

Thomas Moore (1779–1852)

from SONNETS
William Wordsworth (1770–1850)

Our bodily life, some plead, that life the shrine
Of an immortal spirit, is a gift
So sacred, so informed with light divine,
That no tribunal, though most wise to sift
Deed and intent, should turn the Being adrift
Into that world where penitential tear
May not avail, nor prayer have for God's ear
A voice—that world whose veil no hand can lift
For earthly sight. "Eternity and Time,"
'They' urge, "have interwoven claims and rights
Not to be jeopardised through foulest crime:
The sentence rule by mercy's heaven-born lights."
Even so; but measuring not by finite sense
Infinite Power, perfect Intelligence.

from FRUITS OF SOLITUDE

William Penn (1644–1718)

And he that lives to live ever, never fears dying.
Nor can the Means be terrible to him that heartily believes
    the End.
For tho' Death be a Dark Passage, it leads to Immortality,
    and that's Recompence enough for Suffering of it.
And yet Faith Lights us, even through the Grave, being the
    Evidence of Things not seen.
And this is the Comfort of the Good, that the Grave
    cannot hold them, and that they live as soon as they
    die.
For Death is no more than a Turning of us over from Time
    to Eternity.

Life is eternal and love is immortal and death is only a horizon; and a horizon is nothing save the limit of our sight.

Rossiter W. Raymond (1840–1918)

Death brings us again to our friends. They are waiting for us, and we shall not be long. They have gone before us, and are like the angels in heaven. They stand upon the borders of the grave to welcome us with the countenance of affection which they wore on earth,—yet more lovely, more radiant, more spiritual.

Henry Wadsworth Longfellow (1807–1882)

NOT LOST BUT GONE BEFORE

Caroline Elizabeth Sarah (Sheridan) Norton (1808–1877)

For death and life, in ceaseless strife,
Beat wild on this world's shore,
And all our calm is in that balm—
Not lost but gone before.

BECAUSE I COULD NOT STOP FOR DEATH

Emily Dickinson (1830–1886)

Because I could not stop for Death,
He kindly stopped for me;
The carriage held but just ourselves
And Immortality.

We slowly drove, he knew no haste,
And I had put away
My labor, and my leisure too,
For his civility.

We passed the school where children played
At wrestling in a ring;
We passed the fields of gazing grain,
We passed the setting sun.

We paused before a house that seemed
A swelling of the ground;
The roof was scarcely visible,
The cornice but a mound.

Since then 't is centuries; but each
Feels shorter than the day
I first surmised the horses' heads
Were toward eternity.

HOUR OF PEACEFUL REST
William Bingham Tappan (1794–1849)

There is an hour of peaceful rest
To mourning wanderers given;
There is a joy for souls distrest,
A balm for every wounded breast,
'Tis found above, in heaven.

There is a soft, a downy bed,
Far from these shades of even;
A couch for weary mortals spread,
Where they may rest the aching head,
And find repose in heaven.

There is a home for weary souls,
By sin and sorrow driven;
When tossed on life's tempestuous shoals,
Where storms arise and ocean rolls,
And all is drear but heaven.

There Faith lifts up her cheerful eye,
To brighter prospects given;
And views the tempest passing by,
The evening shadows quickly fly,
And all serene in heaven.

There fragrant flowers, immortal, bloom,
And joys supreme are given:
There rays divine disperse the gloom—:
Beyond the confines of the tomb
Appears the dawn of heaven.

FAREWELL

Thomas Moore (1779–1852)

Farewell! but whenever you welcome the hour
That awakens the night-song of mirth in your bower,
Then think of the friend who once welcomed it too,
And forgot his own griefs to be happy with you.
His griefs may return, not a hope may remain
Of the few that have brighten'd his pathway of pain,
But he ne'er will forget the short vision, that threw
Its enchantment around him, while lingering with you.

And still on that evening, when pleasure fills up
To the highest top sparkle each heart and each cup,
Where'er my path lies, be it gloomy or bright,
My soul, happy friends, shall be with you that night;
Shall join in your revels, your sports, and your wiles,
And return to me, beaming all o'er with your smiles—
Too blest, if it tells me that, 'mid the gay cheer,
Some kind voice has murmur'd, "I wish he were here!"

Let Fate do her worst, there are relics of joy,
Bright dreams of the past, which she cannot destroy;
Which come in the night-time of sorrow and care,
And bring back the features that joy used to wear.
Long, long be my heart with such memories fill'd!
Like the vase, in which roses have once been distill'd —
You may break, you may shatter the vase, if you will,
But the scent of the roses will hang round it still.

JOY AND PEACE IN BELIEVING

William Cowper (1731–1800)

Sometimes a light surprises
The Christian while he sings;
It is the Lord who rises
With healing on His wings:
When comforts are declining,
He grants the soul again
A season of clear shining
To cheer it after rain.

In holy contemplation,
We sweetly then pursue
The theme of God's salvation,
And find it ever new:
Set free from present sorrow,
We cheerfully can say,
E'en let the unknown to-morrow
Bring with it what it may!

It can bring with it nothing,
But He will bear us through;
Who gives the lilies clothing,
Will clothe His people too;
Beneath the spreading heavens
No creature but is fed;
And He who feeds the ravens
Will give His children bread.

Though vine nor fig tree neither
Their wonted fruit shall bear,
Though all the field should wither,
Nor flocks, nor herds, be there:
Yet God the same abiding,
His praise shall tune my voice;
For, while in Him confiding,
I cannot but rejoice.

TIE THE STRINGS TO MY LIFE
Emily Dickinson (1830–1886)

Tie the strings to my life, my Lord,
Then I am ready to go!
Just a look at the horses—
Rapid! That will do!

Put me in on the firmest side,
So I shall never fall;
For we must ride to the Judgment,
And it 's partly down hill.

But never I mind the bridges,
And never I mind the sea;
Held fast in everlasting race
By my own choice and thee.

Good-by to the life I used to live,
And the world I used to know;
And kiss the hills for me, just once;
Now I am ready to go!

AND LET THIS FEEBLE BODY FAIL

Charles Wesley (1707–1788)

And let this feeble body fail,
And let it droop and die;
My soul shall quit the mournful vale,
And soar to worlds on high;
Shall join the disembodied saints,
And find its long sought rest,
That only bliss for which it pants,
In my Redeemer's breast.

In hope of that immortal crown
I now the cross sustain,
And gladly wander up and down,
And smile at toil and pain:
I suffer out my threescore years,
Till my Deliverer come,
And wipe away His servant's tears,
And take His exile home.

O what hath Jesus bought for me!
Before my ravished eyes
Rivers of life divine I see,
And trees of paradise:
I see a world of spirits bright,
Who taste the pleasures there;
They all are robed in spotless white,
And conquering palms they bear.

O what are all my sufferings here,
If, Lord, Thou count me meet

With that enraptured host to appear,
And worship at Thy feet!
Give joy or grief, give ease or pain,
Take life or friends away,
But let me find them all again
In that eternal day.

from REFLECTIONS OF
KING HEZEKIAH
Hannah More (1745–1833)

The soul on earth is an immortal guest,
Compell'd to starve at an unreal feast:
A spark, which upward tends by nature's force:
A stream diverted from its parent source;
A drop dissever'd from the boundless sea;
A moment, parted from eternity;
A pilgrim panting for the rest to come;
An exile, anxious for his native home.

Death to a good man is but passing through a dark entry, out of one little dusky room of his Father's house into another that is fair and large, lightsome and glorious, and divinely entertaining.

Adam Clarke (1762–1832)

Brethren, we are all sailing home; and by and by, when we are not thinking of it, some shadowy thing (men call it death), at midnight, will pass by, and will call us by name, and will say, "I have a message for you from home; God wants you; heaven waits for you."

Henry Ward Beecher (1813–1887)

What is our death but a night's sleep? For as through sleep all weariness and faintness pass away and cease, and the powers of the spirit come back again, so that in the morning we arise fresh and strong and joyous; so at the Last Day we shall rise again as if we had only slept a night, and shall be fresh and strong.

Martin Luther (1483–1546)

Part 3

IN SOMNIS VERITAS: THE TRUTH *of* DREAMS *and* DREAMS *of* TRUTH

What came from the earth returns to the earth, and the spirit that was sent from heaven, again carried back, is received into the temple of heaven.

Lucretius (99–55 BC)

Is death the last sleep? No, it is the last final awakening.

Sir Walter Scott (1771–1832)

from A PSALM OF LIFE

Henry Wadsworth Longfellow (1807–1882)

Tell me not, in mournful numbers,
Life is but an empty dream!—
For the soul is dead that slumbers,
And things are not what they seem.

Life is real! Life is earnest!
And the grave is not its goal;
Dust thou art, to dust returnest,
Was not spoken of the soul. . . .

Lives of great men all remind us
We can make our lives sublime,
And, departing, leave behind us
Footprints on the sands of time.

MARVEL OF MARVELS

Christina Georgina Rossetti (1830–1894)

Marvel of marvels, if I myself shall behold
With mine own eyes my King in His city of gold;
Where the least of lambs is spotless white in the fold,
Where the least and last of saints in spotless white is stoled,
Where the dimmest head beyond a moon is aureoled.
O saints, my belovèd, now mouldering to mould in the
    mould,
Shall I see you lift your heads, see your cerements unroll'd,
See with these very eyes? who now in darkness and cold
Tremble for the midnight cry, the rapture, the tale untold,
"The Bridegroom cometh, cometh, His Bride to enfold!"

Cold it is, my belovèd, since your funeral bell was toll'd:
Cold it is, O my King, how cold alone on the wold!

LINES TO AN INDIAN AIR

Percy Bysshe Shelley (1792–1822)

I arise from dreams of thee
In the first sweet sleep of night,
When the winds are breathing low,
And the stars are shining bright;
I arise from dreams of thee,
And a spirit in my feet
Hath led me—who knows how?—
To thy chamber-window, sweet!

The wandering airs they faint
On the dark, the silent stream;
And the champak odours fail
Like sweet thoughts in a dream;
The nightingale's complaint,
It dies upon her heart,
As I must on thine,
Oh, beloved as thou art!

Oh lift me from the grass!
I die! I faint! I fail!
Let thy love in kisses rain
On my lips and eyelids pale.
My cheek is cold and white, alas!
My heart beats loud and fast,
Oh! press it to thine own again,
Where it will break at last.

REFLECTIONS

George William ("A. E.") Russell (1867–1935)

How shallow is this mere that gleams!
Its depth of blue is from the skies,
And from a distant sun the dreams
And lovely light within your eyes.

We deem our love so infinite
Because the Lord is everywhere,
And love awakening is made bright
And bathed in that diviner air.

We go on our enchanted way
And deem our hours immortal hours,
Who are but shadow kings that play
With mirrored majesties and powers.

ONE AND ALL

Jane Barlow (1857–1917)

O'er boundless fields of night, lo, near and far
Light, dewdrop's blink, and Light, Aeonian star.
Wan wraiths that flickering roam by marish ways;
Fierce surge of levin-bright foam where oceans blaze—
Fly's spark and flame gulfs dire, your fount is one,
Deep in the worlds' arch-fire of all suns' Sun.

A burning seed of strife Fate strews, and so
Life, men's grudged dole, and Life, gods' feast aglow.
Clod's captive, senses' thrall, oft grieved, soon slain;
Immortal, glad o'er all to range and reign—
Frail breath, and spirit eterne, beyond thought's seeing
Ye touch for one sole bourne all being's Being.

from PECCAVI, DOMINE
Archibald Lampman (1861–1899)

O Power to whom this earthly clime
Is but an atom in the whole,
O Poet-heart of Space and Time,
O Maker and immortal Soul,
Within whose glowing rings are bound,
Out of whose sleepless heart had birth
The cloudy blue, the starry round,
And this small miracle of earth:

Who liv'st in every living thing,
And all things are thy script and chart,
Who rid'st upon the eagle's wing,
And yearnest in the human heart;
O Riddle with a single clue,
Love, deathless, protean, secure,
The ever old, the ever new,
O Energy, serene and pure.

Thou, who art also part of me,
Whose glory I have sometime seen,
O Vision of the Ought-to-be,
O Memory of the Might-have-been,
I have had glimpses of thy way,
And moved with winds and walked with stars,
But, weary, I have fallen astray,
And, wounded, who shall count my scars? . . .

I stand upon thy mountain-heads,
And gaze until mine eyes are dim;
The golden morning glows and spreads;

The hoary vapours break and swim.
I see thy blossoming fields, divine,
Thy shining clouds, thy blessèd trees—
And then that broken soul of mine—
How much less beautiful than these! . . .

O Power, unchangeable, but just,
Impute this one good thing to me,
I sink my spirit to the dust
In utter dumb humility.

from LOVE
Robert Southey (1774–1843)

They sin who tell us love can die;
With life all other passions fly,
All others are but vanity. . . .

Love is indestructible,
Its holy flame forever burneth;
From heaven it came, to heaven returneth. . . .

It soweth here with toil and care,
But the harvest-time of Love is there.

from LIFE OF TENNYSON, VOL. 1

Alfred, Lord Tennyson (1809–1892)

Death's truer name
Is "Onward," no discordance in the roll
And march of that Eternal Harmony
Whereto the world beats time.

from ODE: INTIMATIONS OF IMMORTALITY
FROM RECOLLECTIONS OF EARLY
CHILDHOOD

William Wordsworth (1770–1850)

There was a time when meadow, grove, and stream,
The earth, and every common sight,
To me did seem
Apparelled in celestial light,
The glory and the freshness of a dream.
It is not now as it hath been of yore;—
Turn wheresoe'er I may,
By night or day,
The things which I have seen I now can see no more. . . .

The Rainbow comes and goes,
And lovely is the Rose,
The Moon doth with delight
Look round her when the heavens are bare,
Waters on a starry night
Are beautiful and fair;
The sunshine is a glorious birth;
But yet I know, where'er I go,
That there hath past away a glory from the earth. . . .

Our birth is but a sleep and a forgetting:
The Soul that rises with us, our life's Star,
Hath had elsewhere its setting,
And cometh from afar:
Not in entire forgetfulness,
And not in utter nakedness,
But trailing clouds of glory, do we come
From God, who is our home. . . .

O joy! that in our embers
Is something that doth live,
That nature yet remembers
What was so fugitive!
The thought of our past years in me doth breed
Perpetual benediction: not indeed
For that which is most worthy to be blest;
Delight and liberty, the simple creed
Of Childhood, whether busy or at rest,
With new-fledged hope still fluttering in his breast: . . .

Hence in a season of calm weather
Though inland far we be,
Our Souls have sight of that immortal sea
Which brought us hither,
Can in a moment travel thither,
And see the Children sport upon the shore,
And hear the mighty waters rolling evermore.

So softly death succeeded life in her,
She did but dream of heaven, and she was there.

John Dryden (1631–1700)

What seem to us but sad, funereal tapers
 May be heaven's distant lamps.

Henry Wadsworth Longfellow (1807–1882)

I am fully convinced that the soul is indestructible, and that its
activity will continue through eternity. It is like the sun, which,
to our eyes, seems to set in night; but it has in reality only gone
to diffuse its light elsewhere.

Johann Wolfgang von Goethe (1749–1832)

LOVE IS HEAVEN, AND HEAVEN IS LOVE

Sir Walter Scott (1771–1832)

In peace, Love tunes the shepherd's reed;
In war, he mounts the warrior's steed;
In halls, in gay attire is seen;
In hamlets, dances on the green.
Love rules the court, the camp, the grove,
And men below and saints above;
For love is heaven, and heaven is love.

LIFE

Charles Swain (1803–1874)

Life's not our own,—'tis but a loan
To be repaid;
Soon the dark Comer's at the door,
The debt is due: the dream is o'er,—
Life's but a shade.

Thus all decline that bloom or shine,
Both star and flower;
'Tis but a little odour shed,
A light gone out, a spirit fled,
A funeral hour.

Then let us show a tranquil brow
Whate'er befalls;
That we upon life's latest brink
May look on Death's dark face,—and think
An angel calls.

OF WHOM AM I AFRAID?

Emily Dickinson (1830–1886)

Afraid? Of whom am I afraid?
Not death; for who is he?
The porter of my father's lodge
As much abasheth me.

Of life? 'T were odd I fear a thing
That comprehendeth me
In one or more existences
At Deity's decree.

Of resurrection? Is the east
Afraid to trust the morn
With her fastidious forehead?
As soon impeach my crown!

"BLESSED ARE THEY THAT MOURN"

William Cullen Bryant (1794–1878)

Oh, deem not they are blest alone
Whose lives a peaceful tenor keep;
The Power who pities man, hath shown
A blessing for the eyes that weep.

The light of smiles shall fill again
The lids that overflow with tears;
And weary hours of woe and pain
Are promises of happier years.

There is a day of sunny rest
For every dark and troubled night:
And grief may hide an evening guest,
But joy shall come with early light.

And thou, who, o'er thy friend's low bier,
Dost shed the bitter drops like rain,
Hope that a brighter, happier sphere
Will give him to thy arms again.

Nor let the good man's trust depart,
Though life its common gifts deny,—
Though with a pierced and bleeding heart,
And spurned of men, he goes to die.

For God has marked each sorrowing day
And numbered every secret tear,
And heaven's long age of bliss shall pay
For all his children suffer here.

from THE END OF THE PLAY

William Makepeace Thackeray (1811–1863)

The play is done; the curtain drops,
Slow falling to the prompter's bell:
A moment yet the actor stops,
And looks around, to say farewell. . . .

On life's wide scene you, too, have parts,
That Fate ere long shall bid you play;
Good night! with honest gentle hearts
A kindly greeting go alway! . . .

And if, in time of sacred youth,
We learned at home to love and pray,
Pray Heaven that early Love and Truth
May never wholly pass away.

And in the world, as in the school,
I'd say, how fate may change and shift;
The prize be sometimes with the fool,
The race not always to the swift. . . .

We bow to Heaven that will'd it so,
That darkly rules the fate of all.
That sends the respite or the blow,
That's free to give, or to recall. . . .

So each shall mourn, in life's advance,
Dear hopes, dear friends, untimely killed;
Shall grieve for many a forfeit chance,
And longing passion unfulfilled.
Amen! whatever fate be sent,

Pray God the heart may kindly glow,
Although the head with cares be bent,
And whitened with the winter snow.

Come wealth or want, come good or ill,
Let young and old accept their part,
And bow before the Awful Will,
And bear it with an honest heart.

Whatsoever that be within us that feels, thinks, desires, and animates, is something celestial, divine, and consequently imperishable.

Aristotle

Ah, the souls of those that die
  Are but sunbeams lifted higher.

Henry Wadsworth Longfellow (1807–1882)

WEEP YOU NO MORE

John Dowland (1563–1626)

Weep you no more, sad fountains;
What need you flow so fast?
Look how the snowy mountains
Heaven's sun doth gently waste.
But my sun's heavenly eyes
View not your weeping,
That now lies sleeping
Softly, now softly lies
Sleeping.

Sleep is a reconciling,
A rest that peace begets:
Doth not the sun rise smiling
When fair at even he sets?
Rest you then, rest, sad eyes,
Melt not in weeping,
While she lies sleeping
Softly, now softly lies
Sleeping.

THERE IS A LAND OF PURE DELIGHT

Isaac Watts (1674–1748)

There is a land of pure delight,
where saints immortal reign,
infinite day excludes the night,
and pleasures banish pain.

There everlasting spring abides,
and never-withering flowers:
death, like a narrow sea, divides
this heavenly land from ours.

Sweet fields beyond the swelling flood
stand dressed in living green:
so to the Jews old Canaan stood,
while Jordan rolled between.

But timorous mortals start and shrink
to cross this narrow sea;
and linger, shivering on the brink,
and fear to launch away.

O could we make our doubts remove,
those gloomy thoughts that rise,
and see the Canaan that we love
with unbeclouded eyes!

Could we but climb where Moses stood,
and view the landscape o'er,
not Jordan's stream, nor death's cold flood,
should fright us from the shore.

TO HIS SOUL

Alexander Pope (1688–1744)

Vital spark of heav'nly flame!
Quit, O quit this mortal frame:
Trembling, hoping, ling'ring, flying,
O the pain, the bliss of dying!
Cease, fond Nature, cease thy strife,
And let me languish into life.

Hark! they whisper; angels say,
Sister Spirit, come away!
What is this absorbs me quite?
Steals my senses, shuts my sight,
Drowns my spirits, draws my breath?
Tell me, my soul, can this be death?

The world recedes; it disappears!
Heav'n opens on my eyes! my ears
With sounds seraphic ring!
Lend, lend your wings! I mount! I fly!
O Grave! where is thy victory?
O Death! where is thy sting?

PICTURES OF MEMORY

Alice Cary (1820–1871)

Among the beautiful pictures
That hang on Memory's wall
Is one of a dim old forest,
That seemeth best of all:
Not for its gnarled oaks olden,
Dark with the mistletoe;
Not for the violets golden
That sprinkle the vale below;
Not for the milk-white lilies
That lean from the fragrant hedge,
Coquetting all day with the sunbeams,
And stealing their golden edge;
Not for the vines on the upland,
Where the bright red berries rest,
Nor the pinks, nor the pale sweet cowslip,
It seemeth to me the best.

I once had a little brother,
With eyes that were dark and deep;
In the lap of that old dim forest
He lieth in peace asleep:
Light as the down of the thistle,
Free as the winds that blow,
We roved there the beautiful summers,
The summers of long ago;
But his feet on the hills grew weary,
And, one of the autumn eves,
I made for my little brother
A bed of the yellow leaves.

Sweetly his pale arms folded
My neck in a meek embrace,
As the light of immortal beauty
Silently covered his face;
And when the arrows of sunset
Lodged in the tree-tops bright,
He fell, in his saint-like beauty,
Asleep by the gates of light.
Therefore, of all the pictures
That hand on Memory's wall,
The one of the dim old forest
Seemeth the best of all.

DEATH BE NOT PROUD

John Donne (1572–1631)

Death, be not proud, though some have called thee
Mighty and dreadful, for thou art not so;
For those whom thou think'st thou dost over throw
Die not, poor Death, nor yet canst thou kill me.
From rest and sleep, which but thy pictures be,
Much pleasure; then from thee much more must flow,
And soonest our best men with thee do go,
Rest of their bones, and soul's delivery.
Thou art slave to fate, chance, kings, and desperate men,
And dost with poison, war, and sickness dwell,
And poppy or charms can make us sleep as well,
And better than thy stroke; why swell'st thou then?
One short sleep past, we wake eternally,
And death shall be no more; Death, thou shalt die.

It is not strange that that early love of the heart should come back, as it so often does, when the dim eye is brightening with its last light. It is not strange that the freshest fountains the heart has ever known in its wastes should bubble up anew when the life-blood is growing stagnant. It is not strange that a bright memory should come to a dying old man, as the sunshine breaks across the hills at the close of a stormy day; nor that in light of that ray the very clouds that made the day dark should grow gloriously beautiful.

Nathaniel Hawthorne (1804–1864)

For what is it to die,
But to stand in the sun and melt into the wind?

 *Kahlil Gibran (1883–1931)*

I am a part of all that I have met.

 *Alfred, Lord Tennyson (1809–1892)*

To know, to esteem, to love, and then to part, makes up life's tale to many a feeling heart.

Samuel Taylor Coleridge (1772–1834)

from THE TEMPEST, ACT IV SCENE I

William Shakespeare (1564–1616)

Our revels now are ended. These our actors,
As I foretold you, were all spirits, and
Are melted into air, into thin air:
And, like the baseless fabric of this vision,
The cloud-capp'd towers, the gorgeous palaces,
The solemn temples, the great globe itself,
Ye all which it inherit, shall dissolve,
And, like this insubstantial pageant faded,
Leave not a rack behind. We are such stuff
As dreams are made on; and our little life
Is rounded with a sleep.

Part 4

IN FINE:
FUNERAL PRAYERS

PRAYER OF ST. FRANCIS OF ASSISI

Lord, make me an instrument of Thy Peace.
Where there is hatred, let me sow love.
Where there is injury, pardon.
Where there is discord, harmony.
Where there is doubt, faith.
Where there is despair, hope.
Where there is darkness, light.
Where there is sorrow, joy.

O Divine Master, grant that I may not so much
    seek to be consoled as to console;
To be understood as to understand;
To be loved as to love;
For it is in giving that we receive;
It is in pardoning that we are pardoned,
And it is in dying that we are born to Eternal Life.
Amen.

RESURRECTION PRAYER

I am the resurrection and the Life, Saith the Lord.
He that believeth in me, though he were dead, yet
    shall he live,
And whosoever liveth and believeth in me shall never die.

I know that my redeemer liveth, and that he shall
    stand at the latter day upon the earth;
And though after my skin worms destroy this body,
    yet in my flesh shall I see God,
Whom I shall see for myself, and mine eyes shall behold,
    and not another.

We brought nothing into this world, and it is certain we
    can carry nothing out.

The Lord gave, and the Lord hath taken away; blessed be
    the name of the Lord.*

* See John 11:25–36; Job 19:25–27; 1 Timothy 6:7; and Job 1:21

A PRAYER FOR THE DEAD

God our Father,
Your power brings us to birth,
Your providence guides our lives,
and by Your command we return to dust.

Lord, those who die still live in Your presence,
their lives change but do not end.
I pray in hope for my family,
relatives and friends,
and for all the dead known to You alone.

In company with Christ,
Who died and now lives,
may they rejoice in Your kingdom,
where all our tears are wiped away.
Unite us together again in one family,
To sing Your praise forever and ever.

Amen.

LORD OF ALL, WE PRAISE YOU

Lord of all, we praise you
for all who have entered into their rest
and reached the promised land where you are seen
    face to face.
Give us grace to follow in their footsteps
as they followed in the way of your Son.
Thank you for the memory of those you have called
    to yourself:
by each memory, turn our hearts from things seen to
    things unseen,
and lead us till we come to the eternal rest
you have prepared for your people,
through Jesus Christ our Lord.

Amen.

PSALM 23

The Lord is my shepherd; I shall not want.

He maketh me to lie down in green pastures: he leadeth me beside the still waters.

He restoreth my soul: he leadeth me in the paths of righteousness for his name's sake.

Yea, though I walk through the valley of the shadow of death, I will fear no evil: for thou art with me; thy rod and thy staff they comfort me.

Thou preparest a table before me in the presence of mine enemies: thou anointest my head with oil; my cup runneth over.

Surely goodness and mercy shall follow me all the days of my life: and I will dwell in the house of the Lord for ever.

Index

Bibliography

Ballou, Maturin M., comp. *Edge-Tools of Speech*. Boston: Ticknor and Company, 1886.

Bartlett, John, comp. *Familiar Quotations*, 10th ed, rev. and enl. by Nathan Haskell Dole. Boston: Little, Brown, 1919.

Browning, Elizabeth Barrett. "He Giveth His Beloved Sleep." Boston: Lee and Shepard Publishers, 1882.

Bryan, William Jennings, ed. *The World's Famous Orations*. New York: Funk and Wagnalls, 1906.

Burns, Robert. *Poems and Songs*. Vol. VI. The Harvard Classics. New York: P.F. Collier & Son, 1909–14.

Butler, Samuel. *The Notebooks of Samuel Butler*. London: A. C. Fifield, 1912.

Campbell, Thomas. *The Poems of Thomas Campbell*. Chicago: M. A. Donoue & Co., n.d.

Dickinson, Emily. *The Complete Poems of Emily Dickinson*. Boston: Little, Brown, 1924.

Douglas, Charles Noel, ed. *Forty Thousand Quotations: Prose and Poetical*. New York: Halcyon House, 1917.

Eliot, Charles W., ed. *English Essays: From Sir Philip Sidney to Macaulay.* Vol. 27. The Harvard Classics. New York: P. F. Collier & Son, 1910.

Lounsbury, Thomas R., ed. *Yale Book of American Verse.* New Haven: Yale University Press, 1912.

Milton, John. *The Complete Poems of John Milton.* Vol. IV. The Harvard Classics. Charles W. Eliot, ed. New York: P. F. Collier & Son, 1909.

Morley, Christopher, ed. *Modern Essays.* New York: Harcourt, Brace, 1921.

Nicholson, D. H. S., and Lee, A. H. E., eds. *The Oxford Book of English Mystical Verse.* Oxford: The Clarendon Press, 1917.

Palgrave, Francis T. *The Golden Treasury.* London: Macmillan, 1875.

Penn, William. *Fruits of Solitude, In Reflections and Maxims Relating to the Conduct of Human Life.* Philadelphia: Henry Longstreth, 1877.

"Prayer of St. Francis of Assisi." Trans. from the original French, La Clochette, 1912.

Quiller-Couch, Arthur Thomas, Sir. *The Oxford Book of English Verse.* Oxford: Clarendon, 1919.

Rittenhouse, Jessie B., ed. *The Little Book of Modern Verse.* Boston: Houghton Mifflin, 1917.

Russell, George William. *Collected Poems by A. E.* London: Macmillan, 1913.

Stanley, Bessie. "What Constitutes Success." *Lincoln Sentinel,* 1905.

Stedman, Edmund Clarence, ed. *A Victorian Anthology, 1837–1895.* Cambridge: Riverside Press, 1895.

Stedman, Edmund Clarence, ed. *An American Anthology, 1787–1900.* Boston: Houghton Mifflin, 1900.

Holy Bible, King James Version.

Untermeyer, Louis. *Modern American Poetry.* New York: Harcourt, Brace and Howe, 1919.

Vaughan, Henry. *The Poems of Henry Vaughan, Silurist.* Vol 1. E. K. Chambers, Ed. London, Lawrence & Bullen Ltd., 1896.

Whitman, Walt. *Prose Works.* Philadelphia: David McKay, 1892.

Wordsworth, William. *The Complete Poetical Works.* London: Macmillan, 1888.

ABOUT *the* AUTHOR

Shersta Chabot grew up in Utah, the oldest in a family of eleven children. After working for several years in both corporate and small business accounting, she returned to her first love—English literature—and completed her bachelor's degree at Utah Valley University while working as acquisitions editor for a local trade publishing company. Currently, she lives with her three children in Phoenix, Arizona, where she has taken on the dual challenges of graduate student and teacher of writing at Arizona State University. Shersta is the author of *The Symbols of Christmas*.